Photography of Tom & Pat Leeson
Foreword by Tom Leeson

Right: Sleek orcas, or killer whales, practice their synchronized swimming in the waters of the Pacific Northwest.

Title page: The leggy American avocet uses its uniquely curved bill to dislodge aquatic insects and crustaceans from the shallow waters where it feeds.

Front cover: Solitary and generally unsociable, bull moose rely on willows to provide the great majority of their winter diet.

Back cover: (top left) Grizzly bear sow with cub. (bottom left) Humpback whale. (right) Western spotted towhee.

ISBN: 1-56037-272-9

For more information on our books write: Farcountry Press, P.O. Box 5630, Helena, MT 59604, call (800) 821-3874, or visit www.farcountrypress.com

Created, produced, and designed in the United States. Printed in Korea.

Foreword

by Tom Leeson

Powerful currents pushed against my thighs and threatened to dampen the contents of the wallet in my hip pocket. I fought for balance on the slippery, algae-covered rocks that made every step a risk in this rain-swollen river. I could not afford even the smallest slip as I held on tightly to my mother's hand. I was a young teen, only slightly taller than she, and she was my driver, my transportation to this remote rain forest river on Washington's Olympic Peninsula. Terrified of water, she clung desperately to my hand as we crossed and recrossed the upper Queets River fishing for steelhead.

Slogging through an overgrown meadow near an early-1900s homestead, we came upon a herd of Roosevelt elk. We held our breath as we walked on, our rain slickers swishing at every step. The elk continued to graze undisturbed in our presence. At one point I could have touched one with my fishing rod.

Above: This young red fox in the Dungeness Valley gives the camera a quizzical stare.

Facing page: A western tiger swallowtail pauses on Indian paintbrush.

As soon as I got my driver's license, I returned often to the fast-flowing, pure rivers of the Olympic Peninsula's rain forests. The Hoh, the Bogachiel, and the Queets Rivers became my retreat, my private world. I spent days at a time discovering the haunts of the wild steelhead: the quiet pools at the tail of shallow riffles, the long swift runs, or the deep holes next to partly submerged logs. Names like the old stump hole, Smith Ranch, and Tsleechy Creek peppered my conversations in the same way the names of rock musicians and movie stars fell off the lips of my fellow classmates. Sometimes I went with my parents or a friend, but more often as I grew older, I went alone.

While fishing, I learned where the elk bedded down midday and how to attract an old bull by imitating his bugle in the fall, how to follow the low vibrations through the woods to locate a ruffed grouse performing his spring ritual on his drumming log, how to spot a small fawn in the duff of an overgrown alder bottom. One day while walking a trail, fishing rod in hand, I felt a presence and turned in time to see a cougar on the trail behind me. We gazed at each other for a few seconds before he slipped silently into the underbrush.

I did not realize the education I was acquiring in the rain forest would become even more valuable to my future than the one I was missing by skipping classes to be out in these woods. Little did I know this understanding and deep connection with Washington's wildlife held the key to my future.

On our first date, Pat and I hiked sun-drenched ridges in the Blue Mountains looking for bighorn sheep. We honeymooned miles up the Queets River, camping among giant rain forest spruce and hemlock. Our first anniversary was celebrated while hiking through alpine meadows and late-melting snow fields on the Hayden Pass between the Dosewalips and Elwah Rivers.

My educational pursuits took me to Willamette University's law program. Slowly I realized becoming an attorney meant being indoors with people all day, every day. This was the year Pat and I began our wildlife photography career. After a short stint in Yellowstone National Park, we moved to Port Angeles to have quick access to the animals of Olympic National Park. Because we did not have money to travel, we photographed the species at hand over and over in all seasons and weather, recording the behavior cycle of their lives. In time *National Wildlife* and other outdoor magazines printed our photo stories on mountain goats, ruffed grouse, marmots, harlequin ducks, and black bears. These wildlife studies defined our photo style. We still do our best work when we focus on one or two species at a time and photograph them in depth over many weeks.

Since those early years our quest for new wildlife subjects to photograph has taken us far beyond the West—giant pandas in China, Bengal tigers and one-horned rhinos in India, elephants, wildebeests, and lions in Africa, penquins in Antarctica. But we still choose to live in Washington.

Few states can compete with the wild diversity of Washington. One can watch otters play near the sea stacks out from Lake Ozette, spot orca whales breaching against an evening sky in the San Juan Islands, climb over rocky ridges with mountain goats on the slopes of Mt. Rainier, set a book down on top of a rattlesnake while photographing a prairie falcon's nest in the Columbia Basin, or observe bald eagles stealing salmon from each other on a frosty morning on the Skagit. After twenty-five years of shooting, we still feel we have only scratched the surface of the wildlife potential here in Washington.

It is Washington's amazing physical features that give rise to its wildlife diversity. The Pacific Ocean lends its moisture and temperate climate to create a rain forest and lush old-growth environment on the west slope of the Olympic ranges. Rainfalls of 160 inches (over 13 feet!) make it the wettest spot in the lower forty-eight states. As the ocean's moisture rolls past Puget Sound and encounters the steep summits of the Cascade Range, it creates the heaviest annual snow fall in the contiguous United States. On the southeast side in the rain shadow of the Cascade Mountains lies the Columbia Plateau, a basin of vast lava flows. Its annual precipitation of 6 inches, volcanic soil, and vast seasonal temperature extremes create a wildlife habitat distinctly different from the western side of the state. The Rocky Mountain chain with its specific flora and fauna cuts across Washington's northeastern corner, while Palouse country in the southeast is covered with fertile dust and is a rich agricultural area.

Washington's greatest contrast, and continuing challenge, however, is between our human-based, urban world of congested traffic, deadlines, checkout lines, and tight schedules and nature's rhythms of sunrise, sunset, tides, winding streams, and windswept, sage-covered hillsides. The distance between downtown Seattle at rush hour and Paradise on Mt. Rainier at dawn is only 70 miles as the crow flies, but it is a world apart in mindset.

In spite of exploding population growth and expansion, Washingtonians have always valued the amazing resources Washington contains. Over 10 million acres of private and state lands are undeveloped, including more than one million acres of state lands in designated roadless areas. Besides the crown jewels of the state—the national parks and monuments—more than twenty national wildlife refuges provide shelter, food, and habitat for hundreds of bird and wildlife species, some

in or near heavily populated areas. More than 120 state parks protect from development and provide public access to most of the state's natural treasures. Even within our densest urban areas, one can find places to savor the beat of wings and scurry of little feet so vital to the soothing of ones jangled nerves, a solace to mind and body.

We are delighted our photography was chosen for this book. Our personal history is interwoven with Washington's wildlife. Pat and I have seen our lives' work as being advocates for this wild world that so often becomes lost in humanity's 24/7 universe. As we search through our files selecting photos, we are uplifted by the memories of the good times we have been privileged to spend in wild places observing wildlife—and occasionally even getting a good shot to prove it!

Naturally we prefer to photograph animals in their wild habitats. A few of the more rare and elusive creatures included here—especially the cats—were shot under more controlled conditions. We are fortunate this hand-reared wildlife allows us a close-up view and deeper understanding of species most of us would not otherwise see, yet whose presence adds greatly to the richness and wild diversity of our state.

We'd like these pictures to trigger your memories of the times you've spent with wildlife—and to fan your desire to break away from the hustle of daily life and experience anew the joys of Washington's wild side.

Right: Roosevelt elk bulls, which dwell west of the Cascades, pause cautiously when they hear an unfamiliar sound.

Below: In the open forests of Washington, where dappled light creates shadows in the trees, the stripes of the yellow-pine chipmunk offer it protective camouflage.

Above: A few hundred Stellar's sea lions frequent the coastal and inland waters of Washington. Squabbles and feuds often occur on the rocks of Jagged Island and on the outermost Flattery Rocks on the most northwesterly tip of the Olympic Peninsula.

Above: Commonly known as the fish hawk because of its diet, the osprey constructs an enormous nest, generally near water. While the mother tends the chicks, the male provides each with more than half a dozen fish per day. This osprey, a juvenile, is strengthening its wings in preparation for its first flight.

Left: This raccoon peers over an old fence, ever seeking opportunity to earn its "bandit" nickname.

Above: Though usually seen soaring alone, bald eagles will engage in fierce altercations over territory or food.

Facing page: Chewed stem in hand, a woodchuck sits on its haunches and happily eyes a feast of wildflowers. This charming creature lives in the northeastern corner of Washington in Colville National Forest.

Left: The waters surrounding the San Juan Islands provide the perfect place to appreciate both a gorgeous sunset and a small group of orcas. Orcas are not actually whales, but are the largest members of the dolphin family. They live in small, close-knit pods, which typically stay together for many years.

Below: A pristine snowfall provides a beautiful backdrop for a pair of white-tailed does. The white-tailed deer is commonly seen in creek bottoms and lowlands east of the Cascade Mountains.

Above: The sandhill crane is recognizable because of its distinctive plumage and its almost prehistoric cry. The Conboy Lake National Wildlife Refuge in central Washington is one stopping point for migrating sandhill cranes, as well as swans, geese, and ducks.

Right: These monarch butterflies enjoy a fall treat of goldenrod before making a journey that will take them thousands of miles to winter along the coasts of California and Mexico. GENE STONE PHOTO

Above: A black bear sow has her hands full with three young cubs that are playing follow-the-leader on a downed lodgepole pine; triplets, however, are unusual. Sows usually care for their young ones for about fifteen months, teaching them the skills they need to be independent.

Above: The last light of day washes across a coyote as it stands in a farmer's field.

Left: Great blue herons wade slowly through shallow water or pace the edge of a marsh searching for food. Their diet usually includes fish, frogs, snakes, and shellfish, but as this photo shows, occasionally a small mouse or shrew is on the menu, particularly when ice covers the ponds.

Above: A black-tailed buck and doe greet each other tentatively; the buck is getting his new spring antlers.

Facing page: Olympic marmots are highly gregarious and vocal animals that generally live in family groups of about a dozen. They make their home in the high alpine meadows and on the rocky slopes of the Olympic Peninsula.

Below: Bighorn sheep rams have massive horns that can weigh 30 pounds. They eventually grow into a full curl; the female's horns, however, never exceed a half curl.

Right: Resident of the San Juan Islands as well as sections of the state east of the Cascades, the sharp-eyed golden eagle earned its name because of the golden sheen on the back of its head. Though essentially a solitary bird, it mates for life.

Above: At one time the mountain lion was one of the most widespread American mammals. Hunting pressure, human settlement, and habitat changes have, however, restricted its range to relatively remote areas that provide adequate cover as well as prey. Washington has one of the largest populations of mountain lions in the country, but they are seldom seen because of their nocturnal habits.

Left: An opportunistic feeder, the marten often engages in lively arboreal chases in the trees of the Cascades and eastern mountains to obtain one of its favorite meals, the red squirrel.

Below: Basking in the sun on a summer day, western painted turtles provide a glimpse of their brightly patterned lower shells.

Above: The male wood duck never fails to impress with his brilliant plumage.

Above: A brilliantly colored male western bluebird fluffs his feathers against the cold. Western bluebirds are becoming uncommon in Washington because sparrows and starlings compete for the woodpecker holes the bluebird uses for nesting.

Left: An aspen grove provides the setting for a Rocky Mountain bull elk to begin the fall courtship ritual with an eerie bugling call, usually heard in early morning and evening on the east flank of the Cascades.

Facing page: Raccoons spend many hours meticulously cracking open mussels, clams, and other shellfish. Omnivorous, they also consume berries, waterfowl eggs, amphibians, insects, and, when available, the contents of garbage cans.

Below: Bedazzled by a red sea star, a sea otter swims near the northern Olympic coast.

Left: Smallest of the North American raptors, the American kestrel is sometimes called the sparrow hawk because it was once believed that sparrows provided the bulk of its meals. It can be spotted along the edges of farms in western Washington and in the open country of eastern Washington where it hunts for grasshoppers, rodents, and small snakes.

Below: Because beavers have large incisors that are always growing, they must keep them trimmed by gnawing on bark. Bark and cambium (the soft tissue under the bark) provide part of their diet, along with water plants and roots. In the fall beavers gather large quantities of twigs and small branches to feed on in winter.

Above: Sending showers of sea spray into the crisp air as they surface, a trio of killer whales glides through the waters of the Strait of Juan de Fuca. Several resident pods of orca live in Puget Sound full time; other transient pods visit the area occasionally.

Right: As they have for thousands of years, flocks of elegant tundra or whistling swans migrate south for the winter along the Pacific flyway, resting in places such as the Turnbull National Wildlife Refuge in the eastern part of the state.

Below: A pair of healthy white-tailed bucks in their prime will soon face the hardships of winter.

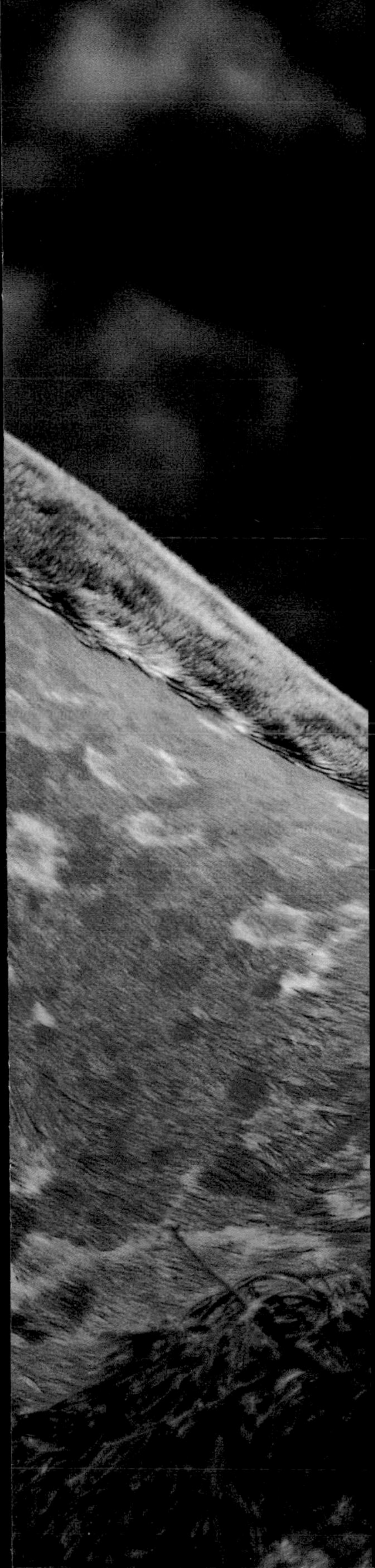

Left: The harbor seal's mottled gray coat set against a lichen-covered rock illustrates a classic case of natural coloration. The harbor seal is the most common marine mammal in Washington, found in all areas of the Puget Sound and even in some freshwater rivers when following a group of migrating salmon.

Below: This cliff-dwelling mountain goat nanny attends to her kid on a precarious rock ledge. Nannies give birth to their young on these sharp inclines to avoid predators.

Above: Visitors to Olympic National Park often glimpse the sociable Olympic marmot, which recognizes others by touching noses and smelling cheeks.

Facing page: A black-tailed buck, its half-grown antlers still covered in velvet, chews contentedly on mountain ash foliage in Mount Rainier National Park.

Right: Porcupines are vegetarians, relying on evergreen needles and the inner bark of trees in the winter for food. They are more common in the eastern portions of the state.

Below: While fish move their tails from side to side to navigate, whales maneuver through the water by moving their tails—called "flukes"—up and down. Humpback whales, occasional visitors to Washington, travel down the British Columbia coastline and into the Straits of Juan de Fuca.

Above: A pair of Canada geese, which generally bond for life, keep their young goslings between them for protection on an afternoon jaunt.

Facing page: Beavers are savvy engineers; in slow water their dams are vertical, but in stronger currents the dams have a curve that increases their stability. Trapped almost to extinction in earlier days, the beaver is now considered almost pesky in some areas.

Below: Turning white at higher elevations in winter, the long, linear weasel requires 50–100% more calories to maintain adequate body heat than its typical plump, round prey. The weasel is, however, thinner, faster, and fiercer of tooth and claw than any animal anywhere near its own weight. This agile creature prefers riparian woodlands, marshes, open areas near forests, and shrubby cover.

Above: Mountain goats like this billy regulate their body temperatures on summer afternoons under the hot alpine sun by lying on late-melting snowbanks. The breezes along these banks provide relief from biting flies as well.

Facing page: Impressive antlers crown the majestic features of this Rocky Mountain elk bull.

Above: Strutting at dawn on traditional courtship grounds called leks, the male sage grouse's puffed-out chest and fan of pointed tail feathers offer a dramatic sight. Agricultural irrigation circles have hurt sage grouse populations in the state, though a few isolated leks still exist in the Columbia Plateau.

Right: An elephant seal bull basks in the afternoon sun; older bulls weigh between 2 and 4 tons. Glimpsed infrequently along Washington shorelines, these massive sea mammals are sometimes mistaken for floating logs by boaters.

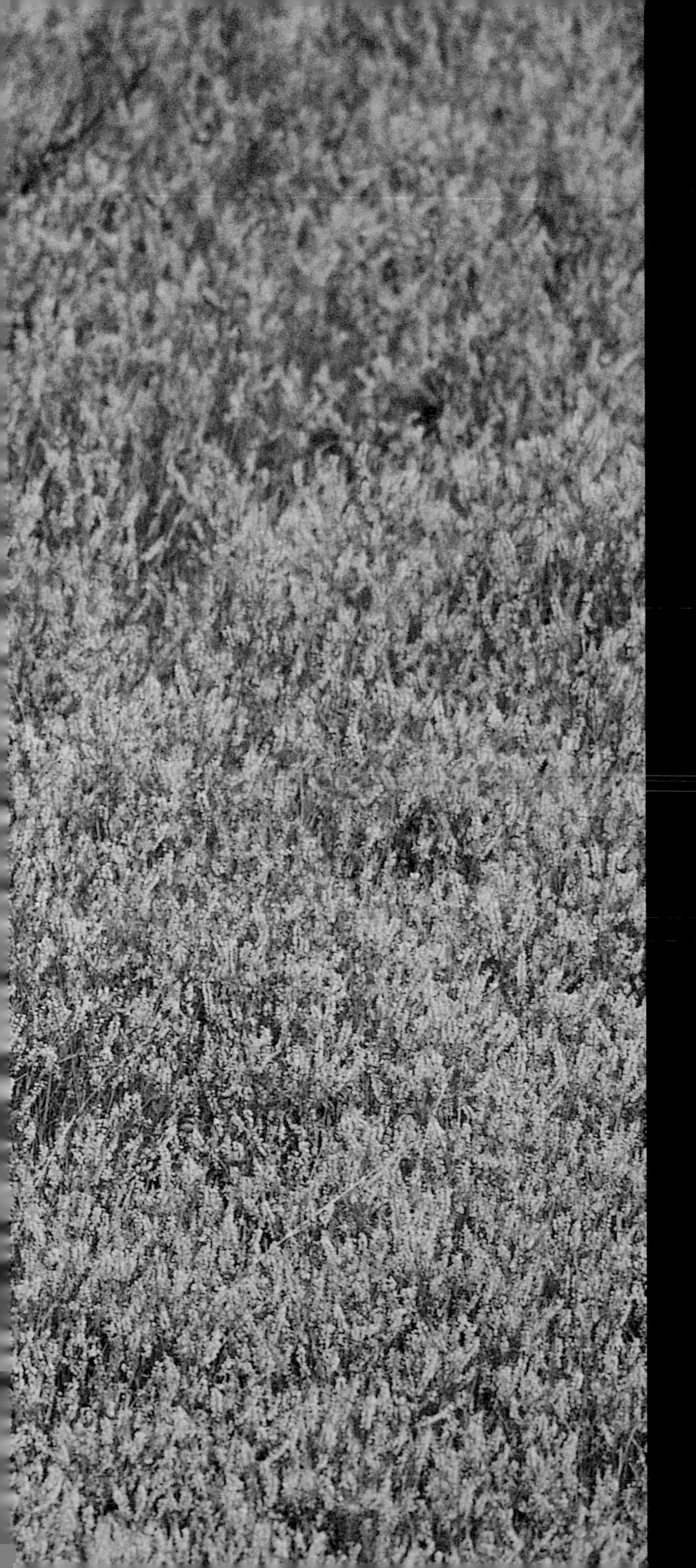

Above: Scanning the horizon with a wary eye, a bald eagle guards its two-week-old young in its nest in a Douglas fir tree. Washington is home to the largest number of bald eagle nesting sites in the contiguous western United States.

Left: A mule deer buck can't resist the temptation of a patch of sweet clover in bloom.

Above: Finding time to play is never difficult for a pair of half-grown badger cubs.

Facing page: During the breeding season, the distinctively colored harlequin duck seeks the pure, fast-flowing streams and rocky rivers of the west slopes of the Olympic Mountains and Cascades as sites for nesting and rearing its young. In winter, rocky coasts such as those in Deception Pass State Park host the harlequin.

Above: An alert mountain lion wends its way down a stream bed in the upper Washougal River drainage in early spring.

Facing page: Dwellers of coniferous forests, Douglas or chickaree squirrels cut pine cones off trees and bury them in food stashes known as middens.

Left: Black bears accumulate significant fat reserves before winter by gorging on fruits, acorns, and other nuts. Huckleberry patches such as this one in the upper Soleduck River valley in Olympic National Park are a favorite bear haunt in the fall.

Below: Perhaps with its unsuspecting prey blinded by the afternoon sun, the coyote prepares to pounce.

Right: The whimsical poses of colorful ochre starfish delight the observant explorer along northern Washington's rocky shores and tidepools.

Below: The western meadowlark generally prefers the open plains and meadows of eastern Washington. Its song is a series of bubbling, flutelike notes that delight the fortunate listener.

Above: The rough-skinned newt, the most commonly seen salamander in the western part of the state, is recognizable by its warty skin and orange underside. Its extremely poisonous skin protects it from predators.

Left: Under the moss-draped limbs of the Olympic Rainforest, a male ruffed grouse creates a drumming sound by cupping his wings and beating them rapidly against the air, which serves as a spring rite or territorial display.

Facing page: Better than a set of antennae, the black-tailed jackrabbit's sensitive ears move to catch sounds from would-be predators such as coyotes, bobcats, foxes, and raptors. These large ears also aid in thermal regulation, keeping the jackrabbit from overheating in hot weather. This hare inhabits the arid sections of southeastern Washington.

Right: A stately Roosevelt elk bull takes measured steps across the Quinault River in early autumn seeking a herd bull to challenge.

Below: A black bear marks a pine tree, leaving behind tell-tale scratch marks that alert visitors to its presence.

Above: Although an uncommon visitor to Washington, the Arctic-dwelling snowy owl is sometimes sighted in winter along the banks of Skagit Bay.

Facing page: This red fox, hunting in the Cascades, might be wondering why the traction isn't better on a frozen pond in mid-winter. As wolf populations have decreased across the United States, red fox populations have adapted and expanded.

Right: Various shorebirds dot the waters of Bowerman Basin on the north Washington coast near Aberdeen. This stretch of shoreline has large concentrations of birds migrating through the area in the spring on their way to Alaska to nest.

Below: The steelhead is actually a rainbow trout that has lived part of its life in the ocean. It must negotiate many waterfalls and obstacles as it returns to fresh water to spawn. Steelhead have recently been reclassified as salmon.

Left: Although snow still covers the higher elevations of Mount Rainier National Park in summer, a group of elk finds plenty of green grass to eat and warm spots for shelter during the day.

Below: The nests of the rufous hummingbird are made of lichens, mosses, and other leaf matter woven together with spider webs. The female takes complete care of the babies; the male neither defends nor raises the young.

Facing page: A strong climber, a young black bear seeks refuge high up in the limbs of a Douglas fir tree in the Olympic rain forest. In western Washington, black bears' coats are pure black; in eastern Washington, they may be various shades of brown.

Below: An orca, or killer whale, breaching is an astonishing sight as it repeatedly hurls its 6-ton body completely out of the water. Orca's are among the fastest swimmers in the ocean, reaching speeds of 30 mph. Very playful, they often perform acrobatic somersaults, tail lobs, and spyhops (vertical half-rises out of the water).

Above: A river otter with its three grown young swims contentedly on a summer outing. Western Washington has one of the healthiest populations of river otter in the continental United States.

Facing page: A Rocky Mountain elk pair share a quiet moment. The breeding season for elk takes place in September. A single calf is born after a gestation period of eight to nine months; twins are rare.

Facing page: A Pacific tree frog peers out from its seat on a garden azalea. It can brighten or darken its skin within a few minutes for protective coloration. These petite frogs often delight urbanites with their springtime choruses.

Right: A black-capped chickadee sits on its perch, surveying familiar surroundings. Chickadees are wild creatures that do not mind the proximity of humans.

Below: Two hoary marmots engage in a playful wrestling match. The hoary marmots of the Cascades hibernate through the long alpine winters, and even in summer they wait for the sun to warm the ground in the morning before coming out to greet the day.

Above: The Columbia River Basin and the northern river valleys of eastern Washington attract green-winged teal for breeding. When ice covers the eastern part of the state, they winter around the Puget Sound.

Right: This large group of mountain goats feeds on meadow grasses and wildflowers on the alpine slopes of the Cascade Range. JASON STONE PHOTO

Left: Silhouetted against the still waters of a lake, a cow moose takes an early morning stroll. She might be glimpsed in the Salmo-Priest Wilderness, located in the far northeastern corner of the state.

Below: Feeling brave, two young red fox kits emerge from their den. Litters vary from one to thirteen young. Born in a variety of colors, from golden to silver-tipped black, they all share one characteristic—a white-tipped tail.

Facing page: The lustrous green leaves and bright red berries of the Pacific madrone tree provide a picturesque setting for the cedar waxwing. Madrone grows vigorously along Hood Canal and in the San Juan Archipelago. JASON STONE PHOTO

Below: Though she may appear inattentive, this black bear sow will go to any length to protect her tiny cub.

Facing page: Capable of killing prey five times its size, the wolverine has large claws and pads on its feet that help it move quickly through deep snow. This largest member of the weasel family is a loner and travels great distances in the most northern reaches of the Cascades and Selkirk Mountains.

Below: After giving birth, this elk cow will spend several weeks alone in the Naches River drainage with her young, protecting it from harm.

Above: An independent young wood duck baby instinctively seeks the sheltering leaves of water lilies.

Right: Washington has runs of both winter and summer steelhead, a favorite of sports fishermen.

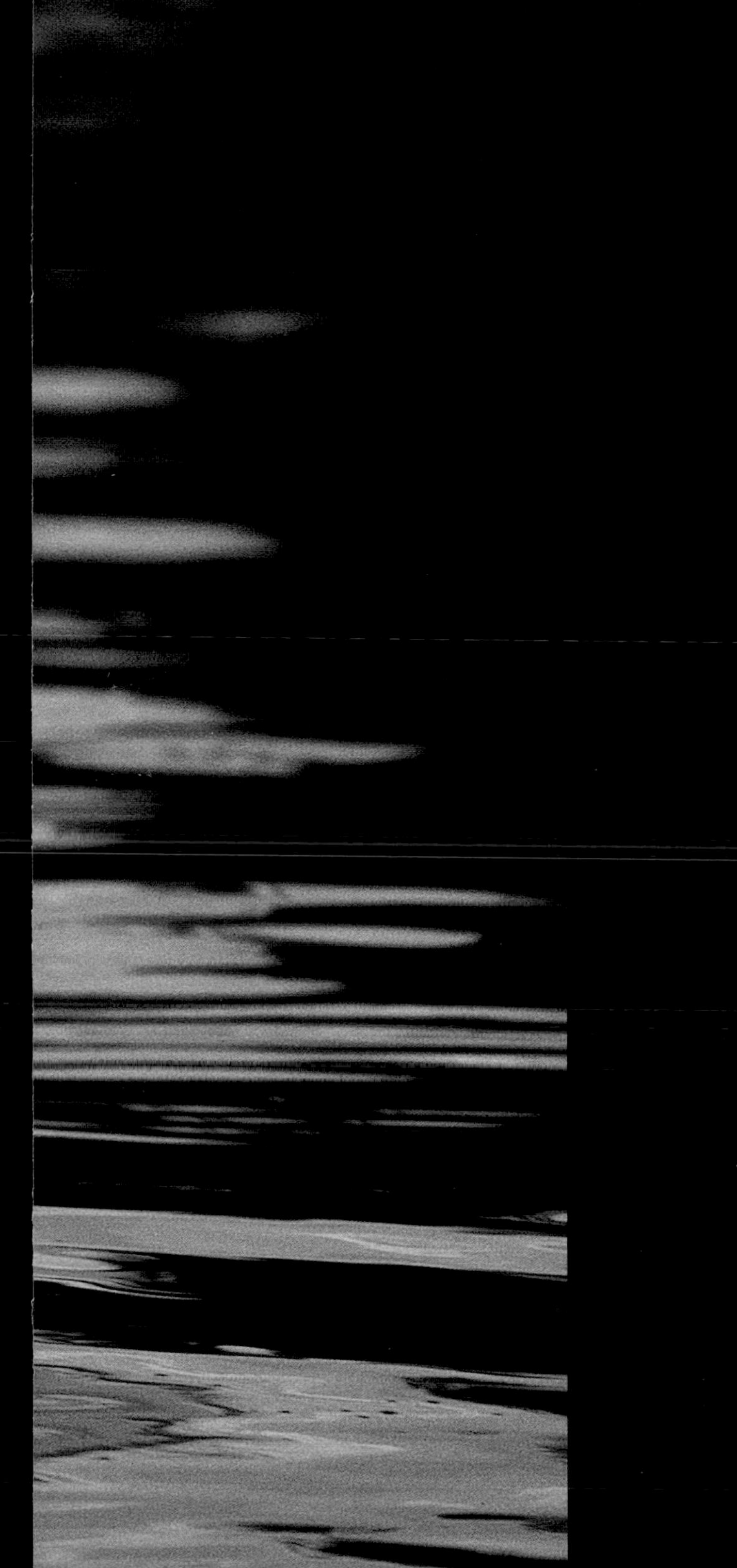

Above: In an ancient ritual, mule deer bucks clash in a breeding dispute.

Left: A bald eagle swoops in for the catch. Though salmon is a favorite, any fish near the surface of the water may provide the eagle with a meal. The San Juan area provides the habitat for the largest year-round population of bald eagles in the contiguous United States.

Facing page: Strictly meat-eaters, bobcats have nocturnal habits that make them elusive and seldom seen, though their range is actually the entire state of Washington.

Below: The Hoh rain forest, with its centuries-old stands of Sitka spruce, western red cedar, and bigleaf maples, provides a haven for the spotted owl. These owls thrive in other old-growth forests in the coastal ranges and in the Cascades as well.

Above: Although this black-tailed deer fawn appears to be on its own, it can rest assured that its vigilant mother is nearby.

Facing page: Found on the talus slopes and rock piles in alpine and subalpine areas of the Cascade Range, pikas spend most of their day foraging for food, guarding their territory, and watching for predators. This pika has collected grass and flowers to dry in the sun in haypiles, which it will then bury in its winter food stash.

Above: A bald eagle pulls a five-pound sockeye salmon from north Puget Sound.

Facing page: The pronghorn antelope does not shed its horns each year like deer and elk; instead, a sheath covering a permanent bony core is lost and thens regrows the following year. In the mid-1900s, approximately 150 pronghorn antelope were transplanted into eastern Oregon. Today only about 60 or 70 remain in a few locations around Yakima Firing Center in south central Washington.

Above: Prairie falcons prefer to build nests on the basalt cliffs above the Yakima River and other rivers east of the Cascades. They frequently recycle the old nest of another raptor. This falcon feeds a ground squirrel to its young.

Right: A herd of Roosevelt elk return to the Toutle River valley after the Mount St. Helens eruption in May 1980. It is estimated that approximately 1,500 elk were killed by the blast, though within five years they had regained pre-eruption populations.

Above: Known for their fierce disputes during breeding season, bighorn sheep rams have double-layered skulls to protect them during battle. Their resounding clashes can be heard miles away.

Facing page: The male cinnamon teal boasts a coat of many colors: rich chestnut, iridescent green, brilliant cerulean, and creamy white.

Facing page: Teeming clouds of snow geese stop to winter in the marshy bays of the Skagit Wildlife Area, just an hour north of Seattle.

Below: The river otter is commonly found in watersheds with clear, fairly deep water and healthy fish populations; Goose Lake in the south central Cascades is one such site.

Above: Bald eagles sit in perfect silence among winter-bare trees. Faithful to their wintering grounds, they return to the same sites year after year. The Skagit River is one well-known place to see eagles perching in winter.

Facing page: Curled up and waiting for the next command from its mother, a pronghorn antelope fawn basks in the June sun.

Above: Named for explorer William Clark during the famed Lewis and Clark expedition in 1805, the Clark's nutcracker pries seeds from pine cones and eats them throughout the winter.

Right: Only about ten grizzly bears live in the northern Cascades. With an additional six to ten in the Selkirk Mountains, the grizzly is one of Washington's rarest mammals.

Above: Although the quills of the baby porcupine are soft when they are born, they harden quickly. Young porcupines can subsist on vegetation within weeks of their birth.

Facing page: A small, isolated population of endangered woodland, or mountain, caribou inhabits several hundred miles of boreal forest and alpine tundra in the Selkirk Mountains of northeastern Washington, Idaho, and British Columbia. They are darker in color and larger than their arctic counterparts and subsist on the lichen of old-growth trees in winter.

Below: A black-tailed buck, with the mountains of eastern Olympic National Park in the background, scouts the surrounding territory from an alpine meadow blanketed with bistort flowers.

Above: Female minks give birth to a litter of three to six blind and naked kits in a fur-lined nest during the spring. The family spends the summer together before dispersing. Nocturnal, they hunt frogs, fish, and marsh birds along streams and brackish estuaries.

Left: A sea otter becomes tangled in a kelp bed. Sea otters contribute to the health of kelp beds by eating the ever-encroaching sea urchin. They wrap up in kelp before sleeping to keep from floating away with the tide.

Below: A coyote pup wanders a river bar on the Queets River, searching for wild strawberries by scent.

Facing page: A determined mountain goat kid about three weeks old crosses the face of Mt. Angeles on a foggy morning.

Below: In areas like the Okanogan National Forest, the snowshoe hare turns pure white in winter. In western Washington at lower elevations, this species stays brown all year.

Facing page: The Cascade Range extends endlessly behind a golden-mantled ground squirrel in late summer. Even though this ground squirrel hibernates through the long winter under 80 to 90 feet of snow, during extremely cold periods it may wake up to raise its body temperature enough to avoid freezing to death. JASON STONE PHOTO

Right: In the coastal woods of Washington, the black-capped chickadee shares a home with its cousin, the chestnut-backed chickadee. They have worked out an efficient system to share the food supply; the chestnut-backed chickadee feeds on the top of the canopy, while the black-capped prefers the lower boughs of the tree. This one is perched in a flowering red dogwood.

Below: Protected from collectors, the red-legged frog is found in low altitudes near cool ponds or slow-moving streams in western Washington. Their populations are diminishing through predation by introduced bullfrogs.

Right: In 1951, Washington's Legislature allowed the children of the state vote for the state bird, and the American goldfinch was their choice. Here one feeds on the seed heads of the balsamroot plant.

Below: A lonely sentinel, this mountain lion is detailed at sunset in the southern Cascades.

Above: A black-tailed doe pauses to nuzzle one of her two young fawns while the other nurses.

Facing page: Shades of orange and gold outline an osprey on its nest against the Columbia River's Beacon Rock. Beacon Rock was named by Lewis and Clark on their 1805 expedition to the sea.

Above: The Chinook salmon is the largest of all the Pacific salmon, with individuals often weighing more than 30 pounds. Washington has four other native species of salmon—pink, sockeye, chum, and coho.

Facing page: The Canadian lynx is another rare and threatened predator that is strongly linked to old-growth forests. One of its last strongholds is the forests in the upper Methow River drainage and a few spots in the Colville National Forest in northeastern Washington. Lynx populations are tied to the fluctuations of their primary food source, the snowshoe hare.

Right: Mallards are known as surface-feeding ducks because of their feeding habits in the shallows of fresh- or saltwater marshes. Although they do not often dive deeply, they sometimes dip under the surface to escape danger.

Below: Common in the grasslands and sagebrush east of the Cascades, the American badger, a powerful excavator, pursues its underground prey by digging with its sharp claws. It can burrow faster than two men with shovels.

A Pacific tree frog eyes the camera as it grips the orange bark of a madrone tree. JASON STONE PHOTO